UNFIGURED HARMONY

A Short Treatise on

MODULATION
HARMONIZATION OF MELODIES
UNFIGURED BASSES   INNER MELODIES
CANONS AND GROUND BASSES

By PERCY C. BUCK

M.A., D.Mus. Oxon., M.A. (Honoris Causa) Dublin
Professor of Music in the University of
Dublin

SECOND EDITION

OXFORD
AT THE CLARENDON PRESS

OXFORD
UNIVERSITY PRESS
AMEN HOUSE, E.C. 4
London Edinburgh Glasgow New York
Toronto Melbourne Capetown Bombay
Calcutta Madras
HUMPHREY MILFORD
PUBLISHER TO THE
UNIVERSITY

FIRST EDITION 1911
SECOND EDITION 1920
REPRINTED 1922, 1927, 1934, 1939
PRINTED IN GREAT BRITAIN

PREFACE

THIS book is the outcome of a conviction that figured-bass, as a means of teaching harmony, has been allowed to acquire an unwise predominance. Every examiner knows and deplores the fact that, whilst a large proportion of candidates work their figured-basses fairly successfully, only a small proportion show, in the unfigured tests, any signs of musicianship. And even the former tests are treated too often as if they were a kind of Chinese puzzle or jig-saw, the results lacking all those qualities of style which practice at unfigured work is likely to introduce. There being no book that I know of dealing systematically with unfigured harmony, I have tried to provide one.

No one will, I think, deny that the first steps in Harmony should be taken in the usual manner, i.e. by means of figured-bass. The nature of concords and discords, their normal relations and resolutions, the value of suspensions, and many other kindred points, must all be mastered if the student is to gain that control of material and tools which will enable him to build ultimately on his own initiative. But such knowledge by itself can only produce a bricklayer, and every worker should cherish the hope of becoming, in however humble a way, a master-builder. In learning such elements by means of figured-bass I would enjoin the strictest discipline, and would exact unbending obedience to the methods of pure part-writing in vogue in pre-modern times. Then the student will be ready to approach work in which musicianship should not only be demanded in every bar, but be held to excuse innumerable lapses from the strict path.

Those who are to use this book have arrived, I assume, at such a point as I have described. If they can harmonize a figured-bass without mistakes, even if without merit, then I believe, from experience, that the kind of work I have provided will help them most rapidly to acquire the sense of style they are at present without. They will find the book practical and not theoretical, and the generally accepted names have been given to chords since, from the student's point of view, nomenclature need imply nothing beyond the convenience of a nickname. To my regret I have found myself obliged to keep examinations in view more than I wished to do; but in this instance, at all events, examinations can claim the credit, by retaining questions of the higher and more artistic type, of forcing the teachers of theory to abandon their old and hide-bound methods of instruction. And I may plead that I have studiously endeavoured to keep out of the examples anything that might look like an attempt to be 'clever'.

The subjects dealt with have necessarily been treated separately, but I think teachers will be wise to allow them to overlap. Elementary melody-harmonization, for instance, might certainly be begun before advanced modulation is taken in hand ; and so with several other chapters. To students I would give the advice that, where the question is printed before the answer, they should think out how they would work it themselves before examining my solution.

Any suggestions or criticisms will be very sincerely welcomed.

P. C. B.

HARROW, *Easter* 1911.

CONTENTS

LIST OF EXERCISES

PART I

MODULATION

CHAPTER I

ELEMENTARY MODULATION

(1) A KEY is said to be *established* when its dominant chord, followed by its tonic chord, has been sounded.

(*a*) It is not necessary that either chord should be in its root-position.

(*b*) In most cases, especially where a tonality is to be insisted upon, the first chord is usually a dominant seventh.

(2) MODULATION is the art of passing from one key into another; that is, of establishing a key other than the one already established, by means of a definite connexion.

(*a*) The crux of the above statement is the word 'pass'. If the dominant and tonic of C major are followed by dominant and tonic of F sharp major, then no modulation has necessarily occurred. There may have been only a sudden *transition*, conceivably faultless; but the word *modulation* implies a connecting link, a pivot on which the mind readjusts itself to a new tonality.

(*b*) In the case of a modulation to a key very closely related, this pivot chord is frequently a simple common chord belonging to both keys:—

Ex. 1.   *Mod. from C to G.*

But for examination purposes, where the object of a question is to discover the point at which a student's skill has arrived, the above solution would be an invitation to the examiners to consider the candidate a beginner. Some such progression as the following is wanted ·—

Ex. 2.   *Mod. from C to G.*

(*c*) When asked to modulate from X to Y, the key X is already taken to be established.

(3) Modulations and transitions may, of course, be made in ordinary composition in any way the writer thinks satisfactory; but in examinations no key should be established except those named.

(*a*) A common form for questions on modulation is :—'Pass from X to Y by means of four chords.' Here the first chord is necessarily X, the last Y, the third the dominant of Y, and the second is intended to be the pivot chord.

(*b*) Ex. 3, although beginning with a transition to F minor, would possibly be accepted by examiners; but the wise candidate will not trust to luck.

Ex. 3.   *Mod. from C to E flat.*

(4) In approaching a given problem in modulation, the essential chord to bear in mind is the dominant chord of the new key; e. g. in passing from F to A flat, first call to mind

an E flat in the bass, with either a $\frac{6}{4}$, a $\frac{5}{3}$, or a dominant 7th over it :—

Ex. 4.   *Mod. from F to A flat.*

EXERCISES.

Modulate, by means of four chords, from :—

1. C to A minor.
2. D to F.
3. E minor to C.
4. F to A minor.
5. G to E flat.
6. C minor to G.
7. G to B.
8. F minor to A flat.

(5) Assuming the student has now acquired some notion of how to set to work, he should aim at making his knowledge of the subject more systematic. Modulations are always classed as Diatonic, Chromatic, or Enharmonic. *Diatonic* are those in which the pivot chord is diatonic to both keys, or to either of them. *Chromatic* are those where the pivot chord is a chromatic chord whichever key we assume it to belong to. *Enharmonic* are those where at least one note in the pivot chord is common to both keys (though not necessarily to the *scale* of both keys), but under a different name.

(6) DIATONIC MODULATIONS are of three kinds :—

(*a*) Where the pivot chord is diatonic in both keys.

Ex. 1 is an illustration of this type. As it is obvious, and not indicative of any special knowledge of the subject, it should be sparingly used except in genuine composition.

(*b*) Where the pivot chord is diatonic in the original key, but not in the new one :—

Ex. 5.   *Mod. C to F sharp minor.*

(*c*) Where the pivot chord is diatonic in the new key, but not in the original one :—

Ex. 6.   *Mod. D to A minor.*

The above three forms are sometimes called *natural*, as opposed to *sudden*, modulation.

(7) CHROMATIC MODULATION implies a pivot chord which, in either key, requires an accidental; the leading note of a minor key being, of course, regarded as diatonic. It would perhaps be possible to give an exhaustive list of all chords which could possibly be so used, but unfortunately many students would commit to memory what they had better discover by their own ingenuity. But a few hints may be given.

(*a*) Diminished sevenths are extremely useful, though more liable to be over-used than any other chord. It is generally weak to use the diminished seventh known as the dom. minor 9th of the *new* key :—

Ex. 7.   *Mod. F sharp minor to E.*   (Poor.)

It is also weak to establish a key by means of the diminished 7th known as the tonic minor 9th of the *new* key :—

Ex. 8.   *Mod. F to D.*   (Poor.)

The diminished 7th known as the supertonic minor 9th of the *new* key is by far the strongest of the three, and is the one not usually thought of by students :—

Ex. 9.   *Mod. G to B flat.*

(*b*) Augmented sixths and Neapolitan sixths, though they can easily be overdone, are useful and always legitimate ; but the student should, for the present, think of them as belonging to the *new* key and not to the old. The following two examples of their use in the *old* key, from a student's actual paper, show an ingenuity which would have been valuable if it had not been misplaced :—

Ex. 10. *Mod. from C to E flat by means of aug. 6th.* (Misguided.)

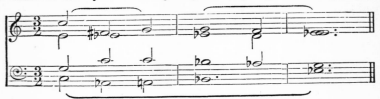

Ex. 11. *Mod. B minor to F sharp by Neap. 6th.*   (Misguided.)

(*c*) The augmented 6th sometimes found on the minor 2nd of the scale, on the other hand, though not often used, may be that of the old key: it is, however, for purposes of modulation, a chord somewhat wanting in 'definition', and so must be used with caution :—

Ex. 12.   *Mod. C to E flat.*

As a possible, but extreme, use of what some theorists would doubtless consider the same chord in its 'French' form we give Ex. 13; but it is too far-fetched to be used under ordinary circumstances :—

Ex. 13.   *Mod. F to B.*   (Far-fetched.)

(8) ENHARMONIC MODULATION implies that some note in the pivot chord, or possibly in the dominant chord of the new key, must change its name either actually or mentally. A simple example will suffice :—

Ex. 14.   *Mod. G to F sharp.*

In the above the C natural of the second chord is, if considered as part of an augmented 6th in the key of F sharp, clearly B sharp. Consequently this is an enharmonic modulation. As a point of scientific knowledge the student should realize that the change is called 'enharmonic' because, in performing it, a voice or stringed instrument would actually change the note enharmonically, i. e. by an interval less than a semitone. Were the last bar of Ex. 14 to be written as G flat instead of F sharp then, by a loose use of the word, this bar would be said to be enharmonically changed ; but in reality it would not be so, being merely the identical notes in another notation.

(9) One point of musicianship may be pointed out. If the new key contains any particular note which jars on the old key, then this note should be carefully withheld as long as possible ; e. g. the note A ♮ is so foreign to the key of E flat that the third chord of Ex. 15 will sound harsh and unpleasant :—

Ex. 15.   *Mod. E flat to F.*   (Harsh.)

By playing a semibreve G in the tenor of bar 2 the progression becomes quite smooth and musical.

EXERCISES.

MODULATE, in not more than four chords, by means of a diatonic chord common to both keys:—

9. From C to A minor.
10.   „   G minor to E flat.
11.   „   A to E.
12.   „   F sharp minor to G.
13.   „   F minor to A flat.

By means of a chord diatonic in the first key but chromatic in the second :—

14. From D flat to C.
15.   „   A minor to F.
16.   „   C sharp to F sharp.
17.   „   E minor to C.
18.   „   B flat to E.
19.   „   C to D minor.

By means of a chord chromatic in the first key but diatonic in the second :—

20. From A to B flat.
21.   „   B minor to A minor.
22.   „   C to G flat.
23.   „   D minor to G.
24.   „   E to B minor.
25.   „   F minor to A minor.

By means of a chord chromatic in both keys:—

26. From C to F minor.
27.   „   D minor to B flat.
28.   „   E to D flat.
29.   „   F minor to E.
30.   „   G to B flat.
31.   „   A minor to E flat.
32.   „   B to C sharp.

By enharmonic means :—

       33. From C to C sharp.
       34.   „   B flat to A minor.
       35.   „   G sharp minor to E flat.
       36.   „   F minor to B.
       37.   „   C to G.
       38.   „   A minor to F.

(The note or notes used enharmonically should be encircled.)

By the chords named (remembering they are chords in the *new* key) :—

39. F to E   by means of Neapolitan 6th.
40. C to D   „   „   diminished 7th.
41. G to D   „   „   dominant major 9th.
42. E minor to C   „   „   dominant minor 13th.
43. A to C sharp minor „   „   dominant minor 9th.
44. A to E flat   „   „   Neapolitan 6th.
45. D minor to B flat „   „   supertonic major 9th.
46. E flat to A minor „   „   supertonic minor 9th.

CHAPTER II

ADVANCED MODULATION

(10) THE previous chapter was occupied with modulation solely from the point of view of the mechanical manipulation of chords. The examples given were mere exercises in the non-musical solution of given problems. But in real composition the object of modulation is to suggest or to establish a new tonality for definite artistic ends ; the modulation being called transitory or cadential according as it is suggested or established. Consequently a student, before considering himself in any way expert, should acquire the power of solving problems in such a way that the result appears spontaneous and musical.

(11) The first step is invariably to use some little figure or phrase instead of bare chords. For example, a modulation from C to A minor might have been shown in ch. i as follows :—

Ex. 16.   *Mod. C to A minor.*

But the same chords can be very easily turned into a musical idea, as in Ex. 17 :—

Ex. 17.   *Mod. C to A minor.*

An even greater elaboration of detail is frequently worth aiming at in order to make the result of more value as music. Ex. 18 gives a new version of Ex. 15 which not only gives excellent practice in composition to the student who imitates it in his own way, but possesses the further advantage of being what examiners, in setting a question on modulation, would like to get as an answer, but seldom do :—

Ex. 18.   *Mod. E flat to F.*

Even if the above is thought over-elaborate, the practice is recommended of beginning with an idea and allowing the modulation to occur, in the course of it, as quietly and naturally as possible. The following version of Ex. 12 will serve as illustration :—

Ex. 19.   *Mod. C to E flat.*

&c

EXERCISES.

Modulate, in a musical phrase of two bars:—

  1. From A to E.
  2. „ A flat to C minor.
  3. „ G to E flat.
  4. „ D minor to A minor.
  5. „ C minor to F major.
  6. „ B flat minor to E.

Also in a more extended phrase of four bars:—

  7. From B to C.
  8. „ C sharp minor to B flat.
  9. „ E flat to F sharp.
  10. „ F minor to G.
  11. „ E to D.
  12. „ F sharp minor to F.

(12) Examination questions of an advanced type generally take one of two forms. Either an entirely original passage has to be written, passing through certain given keys; or a short opening is provided, and the candidate is asked to continue it in the same style. The problem is, of course, identical, since the candidate should provide himself, when no opening is given, with one similar to those usually supplied by the examiner. These nearly always contain some germ capable of expansion and development, and a little practice in making such beginnings will be well repaid; for the poor results usually found in these questions are not due to any failure to reach the specified keys, but to the fact that the whole attempt is laboured and unmusical.

In questions of the type discussed above the modulations are to
be considered as transitory. No dominant and tonic cadence is
necessary in the majority of the keys, though of course one or two
may be chosen for cadential treatment.   Ex. 20, for instance, begins
in C, passes through E minor, A major, F major, and returns to C.
But the treatment is too compressed (e. g. E minor is only hinted at)
for it to be taken as a model, since in questions of the kind at least
eight and sometimes twelve or sixteen bars are allowed.

Ex. 20.   *Mod. from C through E minor, A major, F major, and
back to C.*   (Too compressed.)

(13) That the essential thing is to find a good opening will
be patent after a very few endeavours to work such questions
as Ex. 20 on a larger scale.   A phrase that has possibilities
in the way of imitation and sequences, that can be readily
elongated, that possesses some fairly obvious melodic or
rhythmical characteristic, will be the ideal one ; and if the
interest is not confined too much to the top part, and the
writer is not afraid of rests, then a mastery over this rather
neglected branch should be rapidly attained.

(14) Having decided on the first bar, the next thing to settle
is which of the given keys shall be put in the place of honour
half-way through.   In writing eight bars, for instance, the end
of the fourth bar will naturally, by a half-close or temporary
poise, bring into prominence the key which prevails at that

point.   Consequently the key should be chosen, if there is one, which is reasonably related to the first key.

Ex. 21.   *Mod. in 8 bars from F through A flat major, C major, D minor, G minor, E flat major, D flat major, and back to F.*

In the above the dominant was chosen for the half-way cadence partly because it was a suitable key (though D minor would have done equally well), and partly because the general mistake is to drag in the keys named far too soon.   If the tonality of F is once firmly established and the general flow is satisfactory, then almost any amount of modulation can be got into bars 5 and 6 with far better effect than by overloading bars 2 and 3.

(*a*) If no key appears likely to make a good half-way halting-place, a half-close in the original key is always permissible (cf. Ex. 23, where such a half-close is chosen, though G major would have served equally well).

(*b*) When two keys occur following which are a tone or semitone apart an obvious opportunity for a sequence occurs :—

Ex. 22.   *Sequence through F minor and E flat major.*

(*c*) The key given in questions of this kind are generally related keys which can be reached without having to force the ideas into them; but there is often one outstanding key which looks like giving difficulty (cf. E flat major in Ex. 21).   The attention should be at once settled on this key, and its place in the scheme decided on before the easier modulations take shape.

(*d*) Think out the final return to the original key before putting pen to paper.   Ex. 21 is twice as easy when the shape of the last two bars has been decided on.

(*e*) One of the faults of Ex. 21 is that it is not particularly suitable for performance, except possibly on the organ.   It is unwise to try to write vocally when working advanced modulations, and probably most improvement can be reaped by writing for strings. In this case it must be remembered that bow-marks and phrase-marks are two entirely different things; and also that chords need not be 'spaced' so as to make them easy to play on the piano. Ex. 23 suffers from an attempt to get too much into eight bars; but it shows clearly many differences in style and treatment from Ex. 21 :—

Ex. 23.   *Mod. in 8 bars (for strings) from E minor through C major, G major, A minor, D major, G minor, F major, and back to E minor.*

EXERCISES.

Beginning with the phrases given below, pass through the keys named, and end in the original key after eight bars :—

13. Through G, E minor, F, A flat, and back to C.

14. Through E minor, C major, E major, D major, F sharp major, and back to B minor.

15. Through C minor, G major, F minor, G flat major, B major, E major, and back to E flat.

16. Through C minor, A flat, B flat, E flat minor, D major, and back to G minor.

17. Through B flat, D, F sharp minor, E flat, B minor, and back to A.

18. Through F, E minor, B flat, G minor, C, D minor, and back to A minor.

Using your own beginning, write passages of eight bars, using the following sequences of keys :—

19. C major, G major, E flat, G minor, A minor, F, C.

20. D minor, B flat, G minor, F, E minor, E flat, D minor.

21. E major, F sharp minor, C sharp, G sharp minor, A, B, E.

22. F sharp minor, C sharp minor, G sharp minor, E, A, B flat, B minor, F sharp minor.

23. A flat major, E, A minor, F, E flat, C minor, G minor, E, A flat major.

24. C minor, E flat, A, G, D minor, B minor, A flat, C minor.

PART II

HARMONIZATION OF MELODIES

CHAPTER III

THE OPENING PHRASE

(1) WHEN the student becomes expert he will, after a rapid glance through almost any melody, instinctively know the style, treatment, modulations, &c. most suited to it. But as a means of acquiring this expertness it is better to examine melodies, in the first place, in sections, looking separately at their three parts—beginning, middle, and end.

The Beginning.

(2) Do not begin all the parts at once as a matter of course. Possibly owing to the popularity of choral singing we are apt to think of a tune as *sung* rather than played, and so to connect it with words; and consequently, when writing for parts, to make all the parts start together, as they most probably would if all sang the same words. A very little thought will recall the fact that few tunes start on an accented note; and the note or group of notes occurring before the accent is called the *anacrusis*. When there is an anacrusis it is almost always best to leave it unharmonized, bringing in the accompaniment *after* the first accent, and reproducing in it, if possible, the rhythm of the anacrusis :—

Ex. 24.

Had the anacrusis of Ex. 24 consisted of three notes, then the accompaniment would naturally have had three :—

Ex. 25.

The anacrusis does not always, of course, require such obvious imitation, nor does it always so conveniently allow it; but in most cases at least one part can suggest the opening :—

Ex. 26.

(3) When the melody begins on an accented note it is occasionally best to begin all together. But when the first note is long enough for two chords (Ex. 27), or when the first two notes are members of the tonic chord (Ex. 28), or when the shape of the opening suggests a possibility of quasi-canonic entry by one part (Ex. 29), it is nearly always more musicianly to have some rests in the first bar :—

Ex. 27.

Ex. 28.

Ex. 29.

(4) Do not always begin with the tonic chord (Ex. 30) ; but if the tonic chord is used, do not invariably begin with its root-position (Ex. 28 and 31). Nor is it necessary, unless some definite purpose is to be served, to begin with a complete chord (Ex. 31) :—

Ex. 30.

Ex. 31.

(5) A properly harmonized melody should sound like a composition and never like a harmony exercise. To this end

a student should avoid the besetting faults of such exercises. The most obvious are here enumerated :—

(*a*) Avoid repeating blocks of perpendicular chords, remembering that if the same crotchet appears twice over it is almost always better to write a minim. This fault of style, bad as it is when one note falls to a beat (Ex. 32, bar 1), is unpardonable when the melodic notes are of unequal value (Ex. 32 bar 2):—

Ex. 32. (Bad.)

(*b*) Do not 'tie' notes when the second of them falls on an accented beat unless the musical value of the phrase specially demands it. No one who has ever sung an inner part will deny that in Ex. 31, bar 2, there is a particular pleasure in singing the first note of the alto, which is spoiled if the note is tied. Yet probably three out of four students would, for some undiscoverable reason, tie it.

(*c*) Remember that the ordinary 'spacing' of chords in hymn-tunes and chants is naturally normal and commonplace, and is not to be imitated punctiliously in all kinds of composition. If a chant-melody were given beginning :—

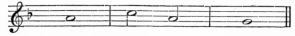

an enormous percentage of answers would be as in Ex. 33 :—

Ex. 33.

Even preserving the ingenuous harmony a far better example of 'spacing' is Ex. 34 :—

Ex. 34.

A course of reading from the scores of string-quartets will help to drive out the commonplace positions embedded in most of our minds by ordinary church music.

(6) A short melody begins and ends in the tonic key; between these two points its object is usually to keep the interest poised in the air, so to speak, in order that the final cadence may have the effect of being not only desired but inevitable. Consequently between the first bar and the last there should never be a full close in the original key, and not more than can be avoided the chord of the key-note in its original position. In Ex. 35 a really bad version is given of what is adequately done in Ex. 36.

Ex. 35. (Bad.)

Ex. 36.

(7) Beware of crowding in too many notes. A melody with semiquavers is a certain trap for the unwary. 'Thick' writing

is always inexpert and unmusical, and is a cardinal fault with organists.   A little attention given to writing in three parts is sure to produce a knowledge of how much may be left out :—

Ex. 37.

(8) If the melody halts appreciably on any note, then is the time for the accompanying parts to move (Ex. 38) ; and such movement should be interesting and melodic on its own account, not merely a succession of chords which harmonize the melody-note.   Vice versa, if there is any marked movement in the melody, the accompanying parts should provide the necessary repose (Ex. 39) :—

Ex. 38.

Ex. 39.

(9) Many accented notes, which rise or fall to the next note above or below them, are really accented appoggiaturas, and

should not be harmonized by a chord to which they belong, but by some chord of which the following note forms a part (Ex. 40 and 41) :—

Ex. 40.

Ex. 41.

(10) Although a PEDAL, in any extended form, is generally out of place, there are melodies where a quiet persistence of one note is often effective for a short time.

(*a*) Sometimes, especially with restless melodies, a prolonged tonic in the bass will bind things together and check any suspicion of aimlessness :—

Ex. 42.

(*b*) At other times such a note will seem wanted in an inner part. Care should be taken to make the ' quitting ' of the note satisfactory. The alto in Ex. 43, bar 1, is made very dull if the minim is tied

to a dotted crotchet. Even as it is, the only excuse for making it
so uninteresting is the compensating imitation in bar 2 :—

Ex. 43.

(c) When the under parts are pretending to be canonic with the
melody, then the harmony is often quite elementary, and sometimes
little can be found for one part except a pedal. In such cases it is
always wise to make a little accompaniment-figure out of one long
note :—

Ex. 44.

(d) The melody itself, especially when set in an examination
paper, will sometimes contain a note of considerable length. A
glance through the rest of the melody, especially at the cadence, will
often give a hint as to the best way to begin. Supposing a melody
begins

and ends with the simple notes

then an obvious start can be made :—

Ex. 45.

EXERCISES.

Harmonize the following melodies as far as they go, in each case adding (with harmony) what you anticipate the next note is going to be.   The exercises illustrate in order the points that have been discussed :—

16.

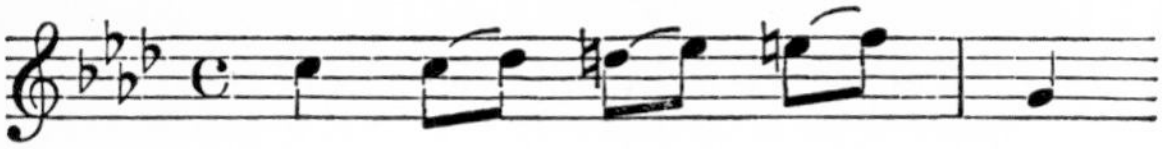

17.

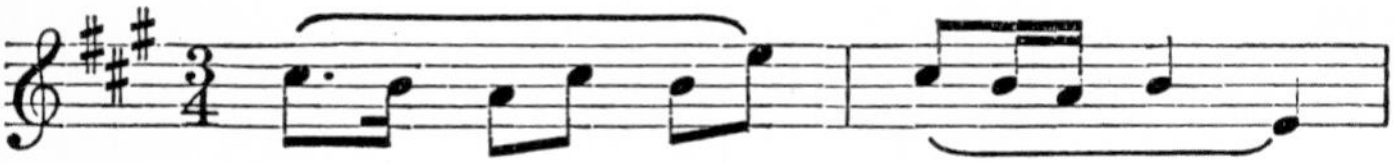

18.

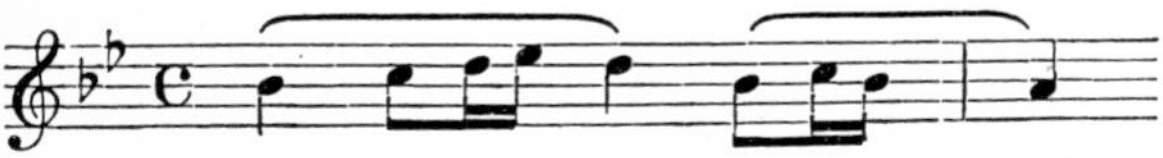

19.

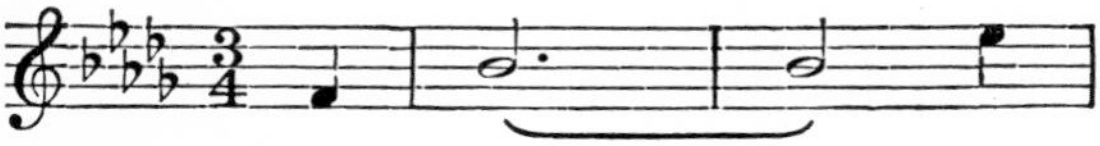

20.

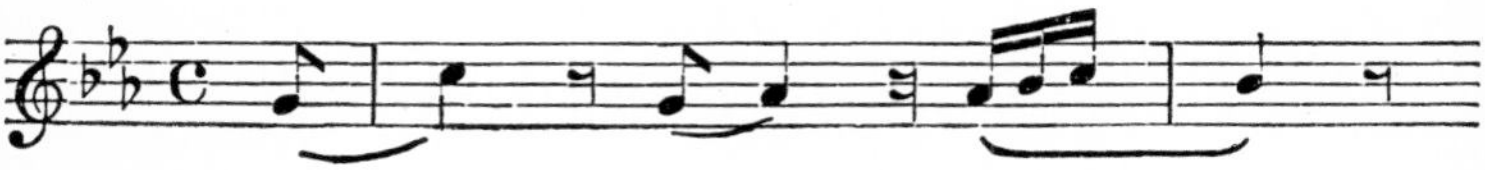

CHAPTER IV

THE FINAL CADENCE

(1) THE management of the CADENCE is only second in importance to that of the actual opening. Schumann has said that if one makes a good start in a composition the rest is easy; he might have added 'except leaving off'. The bulk of the work will naturally take its shape and character from the first bar and will require workmanship rather than idea; but the final bars must be delicately thought out, since they have the power of ruining otherwise good work.

(2) It is almost impossible to give advice on a large scale that will help a student in this task, but a warning against some weak features common to the inexperienced may lead him to discover the meaning of the word 'appropriate' applied to cadences.

(3) Avoid 'ambling' on the final tonic. Ex. 46 is a common form of padding offered to examiners, who know it as the 'village organist's ending'. It is just pardonable in an extemporization if an extra five seconds has to be filled up when the priest proceeds to the altar; but even then it is indicative of extreme poverty of invention :—

Ex. 46. (Bad.)

(4) There are, of course, cases where a final tonic is naturally sustained for some time, and requires artistic treatment, and Ex. 46 gives most of the actual chords available for the

purpose. But some such treatment as Ex. 47 is infinitely preferable, both on the ground of avoiding the cloying chromaticism, and also because, if the phrase be taken from a prominent part of the melody, the final passage becomes an organic and integral part of the whole :—

Ex. 47.

There is no objection to taking the alto above the treble, as in Ex. 47, though in writing for voices this particular specimen takes the alto higher than it should go. The real point is that the student should learn to die naturally and not to take an unconscionable time in doing so; Ex. 46 prolongs the agony of dying, whilst Ex. 47 extends the life of the music.

(5) Beware of reaching the dominant in the bass too soon. There are cases, especially when the tonality has been really disturbed by modulation, where a good dose of chords on the dominant is required artistically to redress the balance; but in fairly diatonic cases the cadence can often be shifted 'a little to the right' with advantage. Ex. 48 and 49 are ends of melodies as they are liable to be harmonized ; Ex. 50 and 51 show the same endings with the cadence-feeling delayed :—

Ex. 48. (Weak.)

Ex. 49. (Weak.)

Ex. 50.

Ex. 51.

(6) Be particularly careful to avoid anything like a full close, with the keynote in the bass, near to the final cadence. Ex. 52, though not positively bad, is not nearly so desirable as Ex. 53 :—

Ex. 52. (Weak.)

Ex. 53.

(7) If, as often happens, the opening of the melody is repeated in the cadence, make a point of reharmonizing it. The artistic necessity for this lies in the fact that the object should be, the first time, to emphasize the tonic key in the first chord or two and then to get away from it; the second time it is to be emphasized in the final notes :—

Ex. 54.

(8) If the cadence is a particularly simple one, inviting the under parts to show some individuality, bring in some characteristic of melody or rhythm. Ex. 55 shows two cadences to a given melody, and several others are possible :—

Ex. 55.

Or,

EXERCISES.

Harmonize the following cadences :—

1.

2.

Harmonize the beginnings and ends of the following melodies :—

10.

11.

12.

CHAPTER V

THE MIDDLE SECTION

(1) ON reading a melody the first thing to do is, as we have pointed out, to form an idea of one's beginning and end. The next is to settle in one's mind what the modulations are to be. The commonest mistake is to assume that accidentals in the melody can be trusted to show the way. Not only do they mislead one very frequently in suggesting a modulation where none is required, but also the most necessary modulations frequently occur whilst the melody remains diatonic. A reference to exercise 10 in ch. iv (p. 44) will show a strictly diatonic melody in F sharp minor, containing two obvious and imperative modulations, to B minor and A major. A melody in F major, on the other hand, containing the notes

will, in the case of a large percentage of students, contain a pathetic but hopeless modulation to E flat major. Ex. 56 is from an actual paper, and was by no means alone in its far-fetched ingenuity; whereas Ex. 57 shows the simplicity of what was intended :—

Ex. 56. (Bad.)

Ex. 57.

Nothing in the world can be said that will help a student to feel what modulations are wanted until he acquires the instinct for recognizing them : but he can be assured that the instinct is one which comes by practice, and that harmonizing at the piano, during early stages, is a great help; and this, coupled with really careful extemporizing, is bound finally to bring success.

(2) Most modulations are to nearly related keys; an extreme key is only used now and then, once in an example, as a point of colour, and only then in advanced work. The extreme modulations always betray themselves by the accidentals necessary in the melody, but as the simple ones do not, the student should be prepared for the following :—

In C major :—

> To G major, F major (usually near the cadence), E major; more rarely E flat major, A major, and A flat major (i.e. to dominant, subdominant, major and minor thirds above and below).
>
> To A minor, E minor, D minor, F minor.

In C minor :—

> To E flat major, A flat major, G major ; more rarely B flat major (when on the way to E flat).
>
> To F minor, G minor.

(3) With regard now to the actual writing of notes, an early opportunity must be taken of warning the student against the use of the $\frac{6}{4}$. As a definite and intentional chord in a composition it has, of course, a proper place, and instances might be

quoted where it is beautifully used as what we have just called a point of colour (cf. Max Reger, Op. 56, No. 1, second bar of prelude, or Scriabine, Prelude in G flat, Op. 16). But when used in an ordinary normal passage the objections to it are as follows :—

(*a*) When used on a strong beat it almost invariably suggests a modulation :—

Ex. 58. (Bad.)

If Ex. 58 be played it would seem impossible that any one could help expecting a close in G : and if the last crotchet in the treble is played as A the demand is accentuated. It is hardly worth insisting on the point that a close such as the two chords put in brackets makes the phrase amateurish and unmusical in the last degree.

(*b*) When on a weak beat the chord is a link between two other chords and is almost equally unsatisfying, and at the same time perhaps more aggravating because it is so gratuitous. There are dozens of ways of writing harmonies under the two G's of Ex. 59 without using the $\frac{6}{4}$ which is so alluring to students in similar cases :—

Ex. 59. (Bad.)

The chord is just tolerable when all the parts move in conjunct motion—e.g. if the first note in the tenor of Ex. 59

had been A—but it had better be left severely alone until the student feels he is expert enough to use edged tools.

(4) Avoid too copious a use of tonic and dominant harmony, even in keys other than the tonic. This might seem an unlikely error to warn students against, did not experience prove the necessity of the warning. When these two chords are used in their original position, as in Ex. 60, the offence is at its maximum; but the example is no exaggeration of the want of musicianship frequently betrayed. Ex. 61 is a better method of treating the same phrase :—

Ex. 60.   (Bad.)

Ex. 61.

(5) Tied notes which fall to the next note are of frequent occurrence. In such cases the last beat of the tied note almost invariably requires to be harmonized by a chord which *forces* it to fall. The original note is not lengthened merely to give it a longer sound, but because it is the point in the time where the composer feels a discord is an artistic necessity. Such a note is the minim G in the melody of Ex. 61, which is, of course, really a tied note as much as if the tune had been in $\frac{2}{4}$ time. Such a note is the E in Ex. 62, and the D in Ex. 63.

Ex. 62.

Ex. 63.

(6) The same advice of course applies when notes are not tied, but merely repeated on a stronger accent, as in Ex. 64. It might, indeed, almost be raised to the authority of a law that, except for some over-ruling and definite object, the chord on a strong beat should be changed ; and even where it is purposely preserved it should be freshened by a change of position and passing notes, as in Ex. 65.

Ex. 64.

Ex. 65.

(7) IMITATION is the life of all true music; but most

students waste an incalculable amount of ingenuity in the attempt to produce exact imitation. So far is this, even when accomplished, from being desirable, that the student may call himself a musician at once when he realizes the true nature of imitation. For reproduction and imitation are two words with distinctly different meanings. To find that a tune will go in an exact canon, or that the bass can reproduce some little phrase with all intervals precisely similar—this is not musicianship, but mere exploration and discovery. Music begins when, feeling that imitation is the artistic necessity at a given point, one alters the unimportant details of the model while preserving the essentials.

The three most important forms of imitation are (*a*) melodic, (*b*) harmonic, (*c*) rhythmical.

(*a*) Many of the previous examples must have been noticed to contain more or less direct references in the under-parts to the melody in use. Ex. 66 and 67, however, will show imitative phrases which are definitely inexact, and are better imitation for being so ; whereas Ex. 68 shows a more extended and canonic tenor which gains in interest and effect from being entirely free :—

Ex. 66.

Ex. 67.

&c.

(Cf. also Ex. 29.)

Ex. 68.

(*b*) *Harmonic imitation* is rarer and generally less important; but in two cases it is always worth consideration. Firstly when, as in Ex. 69, a suspension has given colour to a chord it is often worthy of a reminiscence, though this process sometimes degenerates into a trick; secondly, when some chord has been given special prominence at an early stage it can frequently be artistically reintroduced towards the end. Ex. 69 gives a suspension in bar 2 which seems to call for a balance in bar 4; Ex. 70 gives a beginning to a melody of which the most striking chord is used twice afterwards :—

Ex. 69.

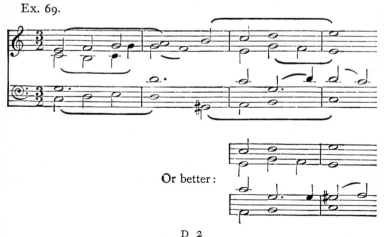

Or better:

Ex. 70.

The use of the key of C major in Ex. 70 is worthy of study, though the return to it, after leaving it for F major, is not altogether strong. But ever since C was the dominant of the Phrygian mode there has been a subtle connexion between C major and E minor which is seldom realized by students.

(*c*) *Rhythmical imitation* needs no special examples, as it is palpable in so many of those already given, Ex. 24, 25, 26, amongst others. Like other points of workmanship it can be over-used till it ceases to have any musical significance; but in places where there is little to arrest the attention it can often be employed without any taint of academicism. The harmonizer who would prefer the first version of Ex. 71 is almost certainly the person who would never have thought of the second :—

Ex. 71. (Poor.)

Better :

(8) It is not a bad thing occasionally to let the melody alone
for two or three notes (Ex. 70); and this is often a happy and
musical device after a climax. At the same time there is no
guide except instinct as to the proper occasion. But a point
should be made of putting this idea into practice because sometimes the more difficult types of melody have extended rests
in the top part, and call for a similar solo in one of the under
parts. This will be referred to later (ch. vi, § 9 *b*) since it
hardly forms part of an elementary discussion; but students
may well be warned here of the danger of thinking continuously
and exclusively in parts.

(9) SEQUENCES are common to all kinds of melodies, long
or short. The fault most common in their treatment is that
the reproductions are made too exact. They are so easy to
write, and sound so fluent, that special care must be taken that
the result is not doggerel. It can hardly be imagined that
a melody so inconceivably trite as to contain the top part of
Ex. 72 should ever be set before a student; but it can readily
be conceived that the harmony given is what would in many
cases be the result. Ex. 73 tries to show that a very little
ingenuity will give even this tag some slight interest :—

Ex. 72. (Bad.)

Ex. 73.

A thing that is often overlooked in dealing with sequences is this : the first phrase should be natural and mainly diatonic, but the notes should be so arranged that the subsequent repetitions, though sounding natural in the context, are harmonized in a way quite different from that which they would have secured had they stood alone. No one, for instance, would originally have harmonized bars 3 and 4 of Ex. 74 as they stand :—

Ex. 74.

Finally, if any suspicion arises that a sequence is becoming dull and manufactured, a sudden and unexpected chord will frequently relieve the situation, and will sometimes even justify the ground having been cleared for its introduction :—

Ex. 75.

(10) *Pedals*, when they occur, are generally at the beginning
or end, as has been already pointed out. Now and then they
are met with in the middle section, especially in long melodies,
but their treatment is for the most part obvious, since some
development of the material in hand is bound to be more
musicianly than any discursive episode. A specimen on a
small scale, sufficiently illustrative for present purposes, is the
C natural in Ex. 70.

(11) Amongst the list of modulations given in § 2 of this
chapter occurs the subdominant ; but it is one which should
be used with excessive care. If it is allowed to occur at the
wrong time it becomes almost an impossibility to restore the
tonality of the tonic. Even an unmusical person can be got
to feel that the following chant (Ex. 76) creates an impression
that the real key is F, and that the chant leaves off without, so
to speak, a full stop :—

Ex. 76.   (Bad.)

If the student doubts the statement above, let him play
through this chant six times, and then stop and think what
tonic is predominant in his mind. An equal amount of modulation to G would produce no mental discomfort whatever.
Consequently scarcely any modulations will occur in a short
melody which require the flattened seventh, but a great many
which travel to the side of the keynote which require one
more sharp or one less flat. In the key of C, the most frequent
excursions will be to G, E (the dominant of the relative minor),
A minor, and not infrequently A major, and D minor will be
found, especially in sequences ; E flat major and A flat major,
since their tonality is far enough from that of C to run no risk

of substitution; but the subdominant should be reserved for one case. That case is when, owing to a protracted stay out of the key and in those keys on the *sharp* side of the tonic, a modulation which stretches back *over* the tonic to the key on the flat side will restore the balance of tonality better than an immediate return. In other words, if in the course of a piece in F so long a stay has been made in C that the mind has really readjusted itself to C as a tonic, then instead of a direct return to F it is often better to touch the key of B flat by means of a dominant seventh on F. And so, until the student feels himself a complete master of modulations it is safe to make a rule that the only good place for a subdominant modulation is at the end of the middle section, in preparation for the final cadence in the tonic key :—

Ex. 77.

(12) A final word may be said on four small traps into which the inexperienced are apt to fall :—

(*a*) Do not use chords in awkward positions till you are sure of them; if then. If you get a chord into such a position by accident then you commit a bad fault artistically; if by design, then it is unwise to try to show off a *tour de force*. The following progression is quite a common one in immature work :—

Ex. 78. (Bad.)

Such writing (and many more examples might be given) is always a sign either of previous mismanagement or of that self-assertion and lack of proportion which thinks originality consists in flouting unanimous and experienced usage.

(*b*) Do not flatten a seventh, even when it is an insignificant passing note, if you can avoid doing so. Ex. 79 is ruined by changing either E into E flat, yet only a small percentage of students would resist the temptation.

Ex. 79.

(*c*) Do not tie a note on a strong beat to the note before unless you have a definite reason for doing so, such as preserving uniformity of phrase (cf. alto of Ex. 80). There are many places where ties are desirable, but the one place usually chosen, i. e. where the second note is discordant and requires resolution, is very seldom the right one.

Ex. 80.

(*d*) Lastly, one of the worst faults possible is the repetition, on a strong beat, of a chord used in the same position on the previous beat. In its worst forms it is not so common that it can be looked on as a habit ; but Ex. 81, a scarcely modified form of the same error, comes from a paper worked by a candidate who, in other respects, had reached a level of considerable intelligence ; and any teacher with a good memory will recall meeting with it on many occasions.   It should need little comment :—

Ex. 81.   (Bad.)

Harmonize the following melodies, using four parts where not otherwise stated, and using strings unless another medium is asked for (the slurs are phrasings and not bow-marks) :—

10.

The Lord up - hold - eth   all such as   fall, . . and lift - eth

up   all   those . .   that are   down. . . . .

11.

12. (3 parts.)

13.

14.

* The examples to which words are attached may be harmonized either as a solo with string accompaniment, or as unaccompanied quartet.

15.

16.

17.

18.

The Lord is gra-cious,   and mer-ci-ful, long -
suf - fer-ing, and of   great   good - ness.

19. (3 parts.)

20.

26.

I will mag - ni - fy Thee, O God, my King, and I will

praise . Thy Name for ev - er and ev - er.

27.

28. (3 bar rhythm.)

29.

44.

45.

46.

47.

That Thy pow - er, Thy glo - ry and migh - ti - ness of Thy

Kingdom might be known . . . . un - to men.

48.

E 2

CHAPTER VI

CONTRAPUNTAL TREATMENT

(1) IN this chapter the melodies will, for the most part, present problems of a character which would have been out of place in an elementary chapter. By this time the student, if he has been through the last three chapters (and has worked the examples), should have attained the facility that makes workmanship more or less instinctive. But it is difficult to concentrate on detail and preserve a sense of balance at the same time. For instance, when specially studying points of imitation, it is right to cram so many examples in a melody that one 'cannot see the wood for the trees'; but in this chapter the melodies should be looked on as complete organisms which have to be set, like stones, in the way that most enhances their value.

(2) It is now imperative that the student should settle for what instrument he is writing. There would not appear to be any reason why, as far as examinations are concerned, the field of choice should not include everything. When no instrument is specified it is customary to write either for strings or voices, though the average candidate never says which, and does not write phrases idiomatic for either; indeed, from the use of C clefs for alto and tenor, voices would seem to be intended in almost all cases. But if the humanity of examiners were only gauged a little more accurately, other instruments would be tried. Even the piano or organ, if a real sense of the technique of the instruments were shown, would be welcome; whereas a candidate who would set a melody for four horns, for two trumpets and three trombones, for oboe, two clarinets,

and bassoon (provided only that the melody showed itself suitable to the genius of the combination chosen) would, even if he failed, have given his examiners a notable and pleasureable day.

(3) When writing for strings it is essential to remember that a slur means a bow-mark and not a phrase-mark. It is quite logical to use both, as Brahms does so frequently. For instance, the slur in the following phrase on a violin means nothing :—

Ex. 82.

No violinist would play the seven notes in one bow, and that he is asked to do. But it may be written as follows :—

Ex. 83.

A study of any string quartet will give a knowledge of how to write bowings, but the important points to remember are that

(*a*) a fresh bow does not necessarily mean a break in phrasing—as between the first and second notes in Ex. 83 ;

(*b*) unless a special purpose demands otherwise the player likes a down bow on the first beat of a bar ; hence an even number of bow marks in a bar is normal.

(4) When writing for voices it is a good thing, especially in any doubtful passage, to sing the phrase to oneself to imaginary words. In setting such a melody as Ex. 84 for voices :—

Ex. 84.

great help in style and imitation may be derived from imagining the words to be ' When the Lord turnèd again the captivity of Zion '.

(5) Should the remarks above result in a trial being given to other instruments, they must of course be treated with discrimination.   A very little study of any book on orchestration will prevent a student from writing grotesque passages for trombones or bassoons ; and common sense will lead him not to overdo arpeggio accompaniments for clarinets, and to make his piano writing contrapuntal, in the style of Schumann rather than Beethoven.

(6) It need hardly be pointed out that free counterpoint is wanted, and not blocks of chords apparently taken from pigeon-holes.   Excellent practice may be had from taking a few notes, such as

and writing passages round them, especially in three parts, where completeness of effect is so difficult.   Let it always be remembered that the greater the contrapuntal interest the less necessary is any special attention to harmony : an analysis of any Bach fugue will discover an astonishingly simple harmonic basis.   *Per contra*, the simpler the melody in non-contrapuntal passages, the more necessary it is to give some small distinction (not necessarily *ingenuity*) to the harmony.   A simple opening phrase such as

in an advanced paper will often be harmonized like a chant. Combining the two little phrases given above, Ex. 85 shows they are capable of a treatment which, at all events, sounds better than the ordinary extemporization :—

Ex. 85.   (3 parts.)

(7) Melodies of the less elementary kind frequently will be more suitably furnished with an accompaniment than with mere harmonization; and such are especially the type that might be set for wind instruments. But the accompaniment should never be of the primitive type which involves the repetition of chords or any form of arpeggio: rather let it be a study in the development of a new and interesting figure :—

Ex. 86.

Ex. 87 a.

Ex. 87 b.

One or two things are worth noticing in Ex. 86.   In the
first place the result of pursuing the first figure throughout
on the two clarinets would be troublesome and exceedingly
monotonous. It is intentionally dropped after three occurrences.
Also it would have been very easy to abuse imitation by
introducing the four-semiquaver figure in many places.   But
that would have destroyed the sense of accompaniment, and
spoiled the effect of the one reference to it in the cadence.
Finally, arrangements of notes are often effective when played
on instruments of different quality, which would sound harsh
when sounded on the piano or voices.   Hence several chords
in Ex. 86 are 'placed' in a way which would be inadvisable
for ordinary occasions, but are quite smooth here owing to the
mellow and blending tone of the clarinet.

(8) Assuming that the student realizes by now the necessity
for contrapuntal writing, he should take pains to give some
point and *raison d'être* to any kind of movement in the under
parts.   Contrapuntal writing does not mean the mere insertion
of a considerable number of passing notes; though this of
course will give flow and effect if properly managed.   It means,
rather, the creation of an organic interest in the whole by
means of relationship to some idea or germ, whether melodic

or rhythmical. An experienced writer finds no difficulty in
providing such a germ: but in early stages it is often baffling
and elusive. However, a careful analysis of almost any melody,
with special attention to the cadence, will generally result in the
discovery of a salient formula. Otherwise one must be
invented, with care that it is not allowed to acquire too much
importance. Ex. 88–90 are three melodies, the beginnings
in each instance being harmonized to show (88) a rhythm
taken from the melody, (89) a figure taken from the cadence,
(90) a new figure invented :—

Ex. 88.

Ex. 89.

Ex. 90.

(9) It will be noticed that in the melody of Ex. 88 a
rest is introduced for the purpose of showing that at such
a point the little rhythmical figure is naturally introduced.
Like all the conscious devices which form workmanship these
short phrases chosen for contrapuntal treatment can easily be
overdone, and then they degenerate into 'tags'. With this
warning, however, it may be said that rests, in any melody, do
not occur because a composer could think of nothing to say,
but because he desired at that point to focus the interest elsewhere. Consequently a rest should invariably be seized on as
a place where the under parts are to show their mettle, not to
'meander' until the melody re-enters.

(a) Occasionally rests will occur at the beginning of a melody.
These are often mistakenly filled up with tonic and dominant
chords, or by a tonic pedal, whereas the invention of a short
rhythm or figure may be of the greatest use afterwards.
Ex. 91 is the beginning of a melody, followed by a working
actually presented; Ex. 92 suggests a way no more 'clever' or
difficult, but obviously more musicianly :—

Ex. 91.

(Bad.)

Ex. 92.

&c.

(*b*) Rests also occur at some length in the course of melodies, especially extended ones. In such cases there is almost always a climax which suggests the right treatment at once: but under all circumstances the passage must be treated as a case for pure composition, and not for 'filling up'. Ex. 93 is the end of a melody for strings :—

Ex. 93.

(*c*) In cases where the imitation is sufficiently prolonged to be considered canonic, it gives point if it is preceded by a rest. Ex. 94 is a case where, though the harmonization is not very good, yet the bass is canonic, and would be quite ruined by having notes on its first two beats:—

Ex. 94.

(10) *Repeated notes*, though not of common occurrence, often bring a student to grief even when he has learnt to treat a long note musically.   A mere change of chord, even in places where the simplicity of the melody demands no more, shows a poverty of invention which can be redeemed by the least touch of syncopation, suspension, or unusual position:—

Ex. 95.

When the repeated note finally falls it is best to make its last harmonizing chord such that it was obliged to fall :—

Ex. 96.

(11) Somewhat analogous to the above is the difficulty of treating a phrase unexpectedly and ingenuously simple. No one acquainted with plainsong can doubt the strength and beauty of the less frequently used common chords, and they should often be preferred to the more obvious ones. Ex. 97 is an ending in which very few students have ever thought of using the chords of E minor and A minor :—

Ex. 97.

(12) It is not unusual, even in advanced examinations, for the melody of a straightforward *chorale* to be given. Those candidates who do not, by far-fetched modulations and other

misplaced ingenuities, torture it out of all its original beauty, usually fall into the opposite error of assuming that, out of kindness of heart, an easy question has been given them ; the result is a chromatic medley or a poor hymn-tune. To treat a chorale as hundreds of them have been treated by Bach is a task requiring the highest skill and sense of beauty ; and there can be no excuse for a student who is ignorant of the Bach versions given in various hymn-books and in such works as the St. Matthew Passion.

(13) A few smaller points, some of them mentioned before, may be collected here, with their bearing on more advanced work.

(*a*) A *long note* in a melody is of frequent occurrence. When it is not merely a pedal (and generally even when it is) the critical moment comes when the note is quitted. This *always* requires thought. When it finally falls it is difficult to think of a case where it should not be so treated that it inevitably *must* fall (see Ex. 43, 49, 63, &c.). But this desire to make it fall is so strong and so generally right that even when it ascends it should be pursued and ultimately caught in the trap which the mind lays for it :—

Ex. 98.

(*b*) Never hesitate to *cross parts*. In vocal writing, pure and simple, there is not much reason for doing so, hence the habit has come to be considered unadvisable. But in writing for strings, or other instruments of large compass, it is most desirable that the different qualities possessed by different ranges should have fair play. For instance, a melody harmonized avowedly for strings, yet containing a viola part which neither uses the A string, nor yet treats the instrument as a bass whilst the 'cello is melodic, might just as well have been written for some other set of instruments, and accordingly loses merit.

(*c*) Make free use of *accented discords*, especially in diatonic passages. Ex. 104 shows a fair number of these, crammed for a specific purpose into eight bars; but any one of them can be effectively used in a single example. Students who have learned to treat an accented melodic note as a discord frequently fail to see that the same treatment applied to notes in other parts is equally desirable. The marked chords in Ex. 99 show alto and tenor so used: in Ex. 100 the bass F sharp is prolonged to receive the same treatment :—

Ex. 99.

Ex. 100.

(*d*) So much good work is ruined by misused modulations that it is worth while to warn students once more as to the care and design necessary in their use. A modulation acquires its value from one of two things, *contrast*, or *position*; that is to say, there comes a time when the mind is a little bored with the tonic key and wants the pleasure of readjusting itself to a new tonality, and another time when, unless a certain new key occurs in a definite place, then the final tonic cadence will not seem logical. Any modulation introduced except for the purpose of satisfying these aesthetic demands is simply 'showing off'.

(*e*) Arising out of the above, we may repeat the advice to treat accidentals as chromatic passing notes in the key more frequently than as notes leading to other keys. In conjunct passages a good deal of interest and amusement may be gained from trying experiments in sounding simultaneously notes which ought to clash. The marked chords in Ex. 101 and 102 do not look as if they would sound smooth, but the conjunct movement in both parts saves the situation :—

Ex. 101.

Ex. 102.

(14) A final warning must be given as to the true meaning of the word *modern*. There is an unpardonable tendency amongst young students to imagine that they bring music up to date by cramming in all the accidentals possible. It is scarcely untrue to say that the reverse is the case. There is more really 'modern' writing in the first eight bars of the voice parts of 'Blest pair of Sirens' than in a volume of Spohr's works. Ex. 103 is a melody set with the request for a really modern harmonization, followed by the working sent in :—

Ex. 103.

The above version is almost as bad as it can be. The parts are unmusical and overcrowded; there is no point anywhere, no climax, no reason why any bar should not be quite different; the chords are all as old as the hills, and the only modern sign (except perhaps the consecutive fifths in bar 6) is the gratuitous parade of them. Ex. 104 gives a version, not by

any means perfect nor offered as a model for imitation
(since it is rather a study in the use of diatonic discords and
the avoidance of modulation), but infinitely more modern and
more organic than Ex. 103 :—

Ex. 104.

(15) *Eight-part writing* deserves a special paragraph, since
it is often demanded in advanced examinations, and many
candidates suffer from an ignorance of the style and treatment
expected. The treatment of the melodies should follow on
the lines sketched above for four-part work ; always remembering that in Harmony, as in Counterpoint, as the number of
parts *in*creases so does the amount of work of each individual
part *de*crease. In eight-part work a part not only may have
less point in what it does, more semibreves tied to minims,
and less movement and general bustle, but it is not good eight-
part writing unless the parts do have these things.

The melodies to be worked will nearly always be found to
possess characteristics which make them suitable for a large
understructure. They will generally lie fairly high ; the
obvious chords wanted will change less frequently ; the quicker
passages of the tune will probably be diatonic passing-notes, &c.

For solid eight-part writing of the very highest order the student should study Parry's 'Blest pair of Sirens'. He will learn from it more than any number of short examples given here could teach him. Let him, for instance, play over the passage beginning 'And the Cherubic host' until he knows the chord-progressions by heart; then let him write out the top part and try to put seven parts of his own underneath it. The result will probably be humiliating, but should be bracing. Real study of the same writer's 'De Profundis'—especially of the twelve-part final fugue—is earnestly recommended to those who find that anything more than four parts is a tax on their ingenuity. Leaving aside the question of beauty, in which respect both works are pre-eminent, scarcely any modern composition can compare with either in the perfection of their strict and straightforward polyphony.

Harmonize the following melodies in four parts :—

Exercises 25–48 may all be worked for the ordinary string quartet: but other combinations are suggested for the sake of practice.

25. For 3 clarinets and bass clarinet.

26. For the same.

27. For 4 horns.

28.

29.

30.
Horn in F.

31. For oboe, 2 clarinets, bassoon.

32. For the same.

33. For the same.

34. For the same.

35. For cor anglais, 2 bassoons, contrafagotto.

36. For the same.

37. For 2 violins, 2 violas, 2 celli.

38. For the same.

39. For the same.

40. For the same.

41. For 6 horns.
Horn in F.

42. For the same.
Horn in E flat.

43. For 2 trumpets, 3 trombones, and tuba.

Trumpet in F.

44. For the same.

Trumpet in B flat.

45. For 8-part strings.

46. For the same.

47. For the same.

48. For the same.

Harmonize the following, first by adding A. T. B. vocal parts, then as solos, adding accompaniment for string quartet :—

49.

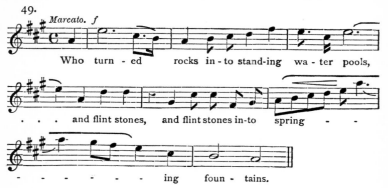

Marcato. f

Who turn - ed   rocks in - to stand-ing wa - ter pools,

. . .   and flint stones,   and flint stones in-to   spring - -

- - - - - -   ing   foun - tains.

50.

Poco lento. p

But my sun's heav'n - ly eyes View not your

weep-ing, That now lies sleep-ing, Soft - -

- - - ly, now soft - - ly lies sleep - ing.

51.

Allegro commodo. f

Th' e - ter - nal God is thy re - fuge, and

un - der - neath are the ev - er -

- last - - - - - - - ing, the ev - er -

- last - - ing arms. . . .

52.

Andante. mf

Good thoughts his on - ly friends, His wealth a well-spent

age, The earth . . his so - ber inn and

qui - - - - - et pil - grim - age. . .

53.

Commodo. *p*

In - cline Thine ear to me when I call, O hear me, O hear me, and that . . . . right soon. . . .

54. (May be set also in 6 or 8 parts.)

Marcato. *f*

Down let him lie, Down . let him lie, ... and slum - b'ring die, And change, ... and

rit. Lento. *p*

change his soul for har - mo - ny, his soul . . . . . . for har - - mo - ny.

55. Complete and harmonize the melodies of exercises 1–20, ch. iii, p. 35.

56. Complete and harmonize the melodies of exercises 1–8, ch. iv, p. 42.

57. Complete and harmonize melodies which

    (*a*) begin with ch. iii, exercise 1, and end with ch. iv, exercise 7 ;

    (*b*) begin with ch. iii, exercise 5, and end with ch. iv, exercise 1 ;

(c) begin with ch. iii, exercise 6, and end with ch. iv, exercise 2 (transposed) ;

(d) begin with ch. iii, exercise 13, and end with ch. iv, exercise 3 (transposed) ;

(e) begin with ch. iii, exercise 7, and end with ch. iv, exercise 4 (transposed).

PART III

UNFIGURED BASSES

CHAPTER VII

ELEMENTARY (HARMONIC) TREATMENT

(1) THE problem presented by an UNFIGURED BASS is a simple one. We merely have to find what chords were in the mind of the writer, or what chords will do instead. Having found this (which should not be a difficult task for a student with any gift for music) the problem resolves itself into the harmonization of a figured bass.

(2) If unfigured basses were always of exactly the same character as figured ones, with just the figures omitted, there would be little to add to the above paragraph. A series of examples might be given for the sake of practice, and experience might safely be trusted to produce skill. But constructive ability is notoriously less common than analytic; and since there are certain features in figured basses which, though easy when the figures are given, require invention when they are not, these features have naturally been seized on by those who set questions. For example, a bass might begin :—

Ex. 105.

&c.

The above is an opening which will at first require thought. It might take a long time to complete, and finally produce something quite inferior from a student who would immediately solve it if figures had been added :—

Ex. 106.

There are, of course, fifty other solutions which would do as well, some possibly better; but in this chapter it will be our object to point out the principal features which, as we have said above, require that intuition which is not so necessary when figures are supplied.

(3) When a *long note* occurs in the bass, it is not intended, nor is it musicianly, that the upper parts should all have long notes also. Any candidate who, in bar 1 of Ex. 106, had placed four dotted minims, would put himself out of court as much as if, in an examination in painting, he drew his picture with a lead-pencil. Consequently a rule may be made that, when the bass rests on a note, some of the upper parts move.

(4) After such a rest on the part of the bass, it will frequently be found that the next note is one degree lower than the long note. In such a case, the final beat of the long note should be harmonized in such a way that it is *bound* to go to the next below. In Ex. 106, bar 2, a candidate harmonizing the first note in such a way that it did not require resolution would be asking examiners to consider him a tyro. Occasionally, between the note and its resolution, an ornamental note is inserted, as in Ex. 107 :—

Ex. 107.

(5) When, on the other hand, the bass moves quickly, the upper parts should use neither too many notes nor too many chords, as in Ex. 108 :—

Ex. 108.

(6) If a bass note is repeated on a strong beat, or tied from a weak to a strong beat, it should, whenever possible, be harmonized by a different chord on the strong beat, especially where the idea of syncopation is at all obvious :—

Ex. 109.

(7) Just as, when dealing with a melody, the result should sound so natural that no one would suspect any part of being the original, so when dealing with unfigured basses, no one should be able to guess that the foundations were the important part of the edifice. Indeed, it is not a bad thing for a student rather to aim at making the result appear like a harmonized melody. One great help will be to discover any possibility

for sequence; though the warning cannot be too often repeated that hard and fast sequences tend to become a trick of the trade.   Ex. 110 is a case where a small sequence binds into a fairly musicianly whole what might have sounded like an obvious exercise :—

Ex. 110.

(8) The *modulations* must be settled quite definitely before the plan of the whole is decided upon.   The first point to look at is the half-way resting-place.   Occasionally this is a half-close in the tonic, especially in elementary basses : but even here, since the dominant occurs in the bass, the inexperienced hand will often force an undesirable modulation to that key. The next place to look for is the passage leading from the half-way spot to the final cadence.   Here there is generally some extraneous key touched on, often the subdominant or its relative minor (i.e. in C major the keys of F major or D minor).   Two warnings will be useful :—

(a) Do not get out of the key too soon. Ex. 110 will not be improved by making the easy modulation to A minor in bar 2.

(b) Remember that, when a key is touched on, its tonic seldom occurs in the bass. Far more frequently the dominant does so, often wanting a $\frac{6}{4}$ $\frac{5}{3}$ half-close; often, too, the subdominant followed by the mediant. E.g. in Ex. 111 an inexperienced student, if asked what modulations suggested themselves, might say E minor in bar 1 and F major in bar 2. The true answer is A minor and D minor:—

Ex. 111.

(9) Some small hints may be gathered together before going on to discuss more elaborate treatment.

(a) Generally speaking, especially when the bass is moving at all busily, contrary motion between the extreme parts is effective. There is no question of rule about it, and discretion must be used; but the result produces a feeling of stability. The student might well play the treble and bass of lines 2, 3, and 4 of the hymn-tune St. Anne; but the opening phrase shows that contrary motion has not the binding power of a law.

(b) As was said in the case of melodies, do not feel bound to begin all the parts at once. More will be said about this in dealing with imitation in the next chapter, but even when using simple harmony, as in Ex. 106, it is clearly not always necessary to start with a full chord.

(c) Be certain of the *key*. If an unfigured bass is set in an elementary paper which is in the key of A minor, but begins on C,

an incredible percentage of candidates will begin with the chord of
C major.   There is no more necessity for a bass to begin on the tonic,
nor even on a note of the tonic chord, than there is for a melody to
do so ; but the fact that they generally begin that way is apt to throw
the unwary off their guard.

(*d*) If the bass returns to its keynote on an accented beat, use
every reasonable effort to avoid the chord of the tonic, *especially* if
the previous chord is the dominant.   There are many places in
music where, as in the slow movement of Brahms's symphony no. 4,
an insistence on the tonic and an apparent inability to get away from
it is the germ of the composer's idea ; but a student will at first do
well to look on the tonic as the port from which he sets out, returning
to it only when his wanderings are over and he finally casts anchor.

(*e*) Do not forget that *suspensions* and *passing notes* are just as
necessary as if there were figures asking for them.   The problem is
to take an exercise and turn it into something as near music as you
think possible.   In the same way allow bass notes to become passing notes—e. g. the note B in bar 2 of Ex. 110 is happier as a
passing note than it would have been with a really beautiful chord
over it.

(*f*) When the bass jumps from an unimportant note, such as
a quaver, that note always belongs to a chord, and is not a passing
note ; but the note on the last preceding beat, which too often gets
harmonized, is nearly always a passing note, especially when in
conjunct motion.   The marked note in Ex. 112 is not meant to be
harmonized :—

Ex. 112.

EXERCISES.

18.

19.

20.

21.

22.

CHAPTER VIII

ADVANCED (CONTRAPUNTAL) TREATMENT

(1) In ch. vii we were concerned primarily with discovering what harmonies would have belonged to a given bass, had it been given figures. In the present chapter it will be assumed that the choice of chords no longer presents difficulty, and the cardinal object before us will be to turn an unfigured bass into something as much like true composition as opportunity and ability allow.

(2) Almost everything that was said in regard to harmonizing melodies is, *mutatis mutandis*, applicable here. The first essential is that some protoplasmic idea should be found which will give an organic unity to the whole. Such an idea may be melodic, harmonic, or rhythmic ; the *sine qua non* is that it should be distinct and musical. Sometimes it must be invented, but generally it can be discovered in the bass itself ; and this latter course is always the best since, when all four parts are linked up by reference to one idea, the result is more homogeneous than when only three refer to it. Moreover, the development of material given is more economical and more praiseworthy than its abandonment and the introduction of new blood. Ex. 113 gives the bass opening which was treated quite simply in Ex. 106 followed by five possible openings.

Ex. 113.

(3) The above beginnings are only five out of the hundreds possible. They are given to show that the opening, if the result is to be musical, *must* be suggestive. Any one who can extemporize at all would easily continue any of these five openings, simple and unenterprising as they are: whereas Ex. 106 sounds, as to its first five beats, like the mere harmonic exercise it was meant to be. The difficulty should be, when so many openings are always possible, to choose the best; and this would be a very real difficulty did not the bass help us. Bad basses as a rule do not, but it is almost an essential quality in a good bass that it should not underlie the structure like the denominator of an irreducible fraction, but that it should contain at least one factor, however small, in common with the numerator. Ex. 113 is the opening of a bass which continues as in Ex. 114.

Ex. 114.

Bar 5 contains an obvious hint which may be utilized in some such way as Ex. 115 :—

Ex. 115.

(4) Ex. 115 shows the importance of *rhythm* in giving life to a simple piece of writing. Sometimes one will search the bass in vain for a terse rhythmical clue, though a good bass, as has been said, will always have some characteristic worthy of incorporation in the other parts. Hence a figure must sometimes be invented, though it is seldom wise to let the invention really dominate the whole, since this is to relegate the bass to a position of entire unimportance. Ex. 116 is a bass which does not give much opportunity for rhythmical imitation :—

Ex. 116.

The triplets in bar 4 are essential features, and must certainly be hinted at elsewhere. No doubt they *could* be made the kernel of the whole passage, and Ex. 117 shows one of the myriad ways of beginning :—

Ex. 117. (Poor.)

&c.

At its best such work as the above is apt to be crowded and characterless, and it will be better, as in many cases where the bass is dull, to introduce a semiquaver into the opening phrase, giving it thus a physiognomy of its own :—

Ex. 118.

(5) A warning may be given here that rhythm does not invariably mean a dotted quaver and a semiquaver. That constitutes the most elementary form in which rhythm can be injected into a languid subject, but the more subtle forms must not be ignored. Ex. 119 is a bass in which the third bar suggests all the rhythm necessary, whilst the first bar provides the cohesive factor :—

Ex. 119.

Ex. 120.

(6) It is scarcely necessary to insist again on the unwisdom of beginning with all four parts on the same beat ; but it is worth referring to Ex. 120 to remind students that it is as well for a part that delays its entry to come in ultimately with something to say. Imitation need never be strict, and Ex. 121 shows it almost at its minimum. But even here, although such late entries might be unwise in a short eight-bar phrase, yet there is sufficient point in them to justify them as music :—

Ex. 121.

&c.

(7) From the above it will be seen that the bass, especially when imitation is in progress, may well be left alone on occasions. In old writers (and in some modern examination papers), such places are marked 'Tasto solo'; but the student is advised to use his discretion and not to conclude that these are the only places where a solitary bass is desirable. The necessary corollary is that rests may be used with freedom; e.g. in Ex. 120 the omission of the quaver rests in bars 4 and 6 would rob the coming phrases of half their point.

(8) Not infrequently a bass will be found alternating long notes with short moving phrases (as in Ex. 122), especially near the cadence.

Ex. 122.

The key to the problem almost always lies in the rhythm of the moving part:—

Ex. 123.

(9) When the student feels some mastery over all the details mentioned in these two chapters he should apply his utmost skill to concealing artifice and to making a passage sound as if it came from his brain a complete and undoctored piece of music.   As his skill in this direction increases he will find it feasible to make his work considerably more elaborate than in the examples given hitherto:—

Ex. 124.

Harmonize the following basses :—

43.

44.

45.

46.

PART IV
INNER MELODIES

CHAPTER IX

ONE INNER PART GIVEN

(1) THE task of providing other parts to a given alto or tenor is one that is practically confined to examinations. It is none the less, apart from being a test of skill, a much neglected method of acquiring the power of distributing interest. The tendency, even in orchestral writing, to recur to the style known deprecatingly as 'part-song' writing, is a natural bias in those who have never concentrated attention on inner parts, and it is checked by a very little conscious effort at the right time.

(2) In looking at an *inner part* a student should at once settle the essential question :—is it (1) a melody, (2) a part of an accompaniment to a melody, or (3) a portion of both ? The neglect of this question has wrecked the chances of innumerable candidates. An examiner thinks out a simple passage for strings, and writes down the viola part—almost invariably of an unassuming character and capable of many treatments. The candidate then, nearly always, takes the viola part as a tune and writes parts for two violins and 'cello to accompany it. This is ingenuous to the point of stupidity. When a bass is given, you are to build a house on a given foundation ; when you have a melody you are to build a house, rooms and foundations, behind a given facade. But when an inner part is provided you have to plan roof, foundations, and outside walls for a house from certain given and unalterable facts as to the conformation of its inside.

(3) There is seldom or never any doubt as to whether the

model is melodic or not ; a glance at the exercises at the end of this chapter will show that what is meant for an accompaniment can seldom be thought of as a principal tune.   Where the student is puzzled he may conclude that if he thinks a phrase may possibly be a tune, then it must have qualities that could be elevated into melody by skilful treatment.

It is well to remember that writing for strings is almost invariably asked for, as offering a wider scope for treatment. Hence the part given is 2nd violin or viola ; and of these the 2nd violin part is practically always an accompaniment.   A viola part may be expected to be wholly or partially melodic, but a passage in which the 2nd violin is exalted into the place of first, except momentarily, is extremely unusual.   But the 2nd violin part may well be of the nature of a dialogue with the first, a short phrase being followed by a long note which invites imitation of the phrase in the upper part.

(4) Dealing first with those inner parts which we have decided to be melodic, there is little to be said beyond the hints already given for harmonizing melodies.   All that was said as to modulations, passing notes, long notes, tied notes, &c., &c., applies direct.   The one main difference is that with melodies in the top part the under parts have to be interesting and rhythmical rather than of a comely shape : whereas when the melody is in an under part then the 1st violin, attracting more attention as the top part, must have more care expended on it.   In the former case the under parts were generally running comments, seldom accompaniments pure and simple (though in Ex. 86 a specimen of this was given) ; but in the latter case the definite accompaniment form is the more usual.

It follows that the first bar is of supreme importance.   Time spent on fixing the shape of the accompanying figure is never wasted.   This figure will sometimes, as in previous problems, have to be invented, but, as before, a really good model will generally be found to carry some hint of what it may be. Ex. 125–8 show how phrases of obvious individuality may be utilized in the accompaniment. The warning may be repeated that, the more distinct the figure chosen, the greater chance there is of overworking it ; and this is especially true of figures containing rests.

Ex. 125.

Ex. 128.

(5) Though there is a certain amount of amusement and instruction to be gained from writing accompaniments pure and simple, as in Ex. 125–8, yet the *raison d'être* of questions on inner melodies is really that a setting should be provided of which the given part seems a natural and integral component.   And so, even when the given part is an obvious melody, it is often best musically, and always valuable to one's ingenuity, to make the free parts intertwine with developments of some chosen phrase :—

Ex. 129.

EXERCISES.

Beginnings of viola parts to be set for string quartets.

(6) When the given part is clearly not the principal melody, then, as a preliminary, the same steps must be taken as in the case of unfigured basses.

(*a*) The modulations (if any) must be fixed, especially the one at the half-distance, and the one leading to the final cadence.

(*b*) A supple framework of the harmony to be used must be mentally constructed. This may be modified and even completely changed before the ultimate result is reached, but it should be definite in the first place.

(*c*) Even before the melodic features have been decided on the model should be scanned for hints as to figures of accompaniment, with special attention to the cadence :—

Ex. 130.

The four semiquavers in the above, apart from lending themselves to this particular cadence, would clearly not occur in any composition for the first and only time just at the end. They form so pregnant a figure that a practised eye would seize on them at once as a promising piece of material to be used, but not overworked, all through the passage ; and such pregnant figures occur frequently towards the end of given parts.

(*d*) Long notes should not be passed over as easy places, but rather should be looked on as special invitations to musicianship. Here, more than anywhere else, the real musicians will be differentiated from the dullards.

(*e*) Avoid monotony. Rests should be frequent, especially before marked imitation, and pizzicato notes, above all for the 'cello, are often effective.

(*f*) If any *repetition* of a phrase seems to suggest a sequence, use one by all means, but do not let it be commonplace or cheap. (See ch. v, § 9.)

(*g*) A *syncopated* part should suggest fresh chords on accented beats :—

Ex. 131.

(*h*) Do not harmonize too many notes : e. g. when two notes fall to a beat, the second being one degree below the first, then the first is frequently an accented appoggiatura :—

Ex. 132.

(*i*) In Ex. 132 it will be seen that the viola has three notes in the first bar where it might have had a dotted minim. Care should be taken in writing for strings not to let any instrument have dull or unrhythmical passages where it can be helped, though some-times the amount of movement in three of the parts will justify the fourth in cementing them together with a long note; indeed, in Ex. 132, unless the time is slow, it would possibly be more effective to give the viola a dotted minim, followed by a minim and crotchet. But where a long note would appear dull it is often interesting to vitalize it by a rhythm, and to use the rhythm later on as an integral part of the whole passage.

Ex. 133.

(7) It will be detected that in Ex. 133 the melody is derived from a hint in bar 5 of the model. Such a hint is very frequently given; and though in that particular example it was not so outstandingly clear that it could not be neglected, yet there are cases where a student would be foolish to ignore an obvious intention on the part of the composer :—

Ex. 134.

(8) We have given examples of the type of inner melody which has to be treated as the principal tune, and also of that which is wholly or partly a portion of the accompaniment to a tune which has to be found.   There is another type, which is

less common perhaps, but is possibly the most suitable form of
all for the discovery of musical ability. Here the given part
takes some phrase which can be used as the material for the
whole, with the result that the whole sounds like a short
improvisation on that phrase. The hall-mark of models suitable for such treatment is usually the presence of some note,
relatively long, at the end of a phrase with quite definite
features. Ex. 135-7 are the beginnings of three inner parts
with the kind of working suggested :—

Ex. 135.

Ex. 136.

Ex. 137.

Complete the following exercises as string quartets or vocal quartets (S. A. T. B.).

13.
2nd Violin.

14.
Viola.

15.

16.

Sweet as the winds . . that gen - tly fly To sweep the Spring's en - am - ell'd floor.

17.

18.

I 2

19.

2nd Violin.

20.

Tenor.

He hath laid me in the dark - ness, he hath

laid me in the dark - ness, as the men . .

. . . . . that have been long dead.

21.

Viola.

22.

2nd Violin.

23. Viola.

24. Tenor.

O gen - tle death, when . wilt thou come? when

. . wilt thou come? For . . of my

life . I am wear - ie.

25. Viola.

26.

2nd Violin.

27.

Viola.

28.

Alto.

God is light, God is light, and in Him .

. . . is no dark — ness, no dark-ness at all.

29.

Viola.

30.

CHAPTER X

CONTINUED CANONS

(1) *Strict Canon*, in its stereotyped forms, is probably a thing of the past as far as Composition is concerned. But as a means of obtaining command and resource it still rightly maintains its place in the training of students, and most advanced examinations include at least one question on it. The usual form of the question is :—' Continue the following for so many bars, concluding with a short coda.' Then follows a model of about two bars, with two parts in canon and one free part.

(2) It is not intended here to give any instruction as to the actual canonic writing. For one thing, such instruction is always considered a part of Counterpoint; for another, it is a matter of extreme simplicity to write a canon at any length and at any interval. But there are certain aspects of Canons, when looked on as pieces of music rather than as pieces of ingenuity, which generally escape the average student. Some of these, which fall under the harmonic rather than the contrapuntal structure, will be dealt with.

(3) The FORM of a Canon must be logical. That is to say, the sixteen bars (or whatever number is asked for) should be divided into phrases with some organic structure. The work usually done in examinations is, though often correct as canon, a mere aimless wandering about with no balance of phrase, no management of key, no development of the opening, and no reason in the world why it should leave off where it does or why it should not have left off anywhere else. It is *not* suggested that cut-and-dried four-bar phrases are wanted; getting away from these is the beginning of musicianship: but a phrase of definite length must be the basis of any musical subject, and

deviations from this length lose their point unless such a basis
has been mentally established. An analysis of the bar-rhythm
of the Preislied from 'Die Meistersinger' will bring home this
fact. A canon, when completed, should be such that a verse
of poetry could be applied to it; not necessarily a four-line verse,
nor a verse with lines all of the same length, but a verse with
a definite structure which would sound reasonable and intelligible to the ear. Ex. 138 is the beginning of a canon set, and
Ex. 139 is an actual working submitted, with no good quality
whatever except the definite preservation of the canonic form:—

Continue for ten or twelve bars, adding a short coda—

Ex. 138.

&c.

Ex. 139. (Bad.)

(4) A student will learn more about canons from an exhaustive scrutiny of the above than from anything that can be told him.   The mere absence of phrase-marks or bowings is a betrayal of poor musicianship; for it should be as impossible to write music without instinctively using phrase-marks, as to write English without punctuation.   The two things are identical.   Then there is no key-scheme, merely a wandering backwards and forwards in E flat, with far too much tonic chord; there is no length of phrase anywhere; no reference to the original phrase, not even to its rather obvious rhythm; no reason at all why any bar should not be taken out or an extra bar put in; and an absurd little after-thought of a coda with no connexion whatever with its context.   Ex. 140 is a simple working of the same question :—

Ex. 140.

(5) In the endeavour to keep Ex. 140 on quite simple lines
the risk has been run—and it is one to guard against—of
making each part of the canon stop while the other goes on,
as in bars 8–11. It would be quite easy to alter it, but it has
been left, because it is simple and not out of place in small
quantities, and also serves here the purpose of showing what is
a bad fault in many canons. But there are other points worth
attention :—

(a) The sentences are of quite intelligible length. A four-bar
phrase in the tonic, followed by another ending in relative minor ;
two two-bar phrases touching supertonic minor ; six-bar coda.

(b) The modulations are logically consecutive. Tonic, dominant,
relative minor, supertonic minor, dominant-pedal, tonic. Other keys
might quite naturally have been introduced, and are sometimes (as
in questions on modulation) asked for. But the guileless nature of
the model does not demand any startling colour in the way of
extraneous modulation.

(*c*) In bar 10 an accidental is introduced in the second part which was not present in the first. This is *always* allowable, and is one of the main methods (especially in canons at the octave) of reaching a new key :—

Ex. 141.

An interesting study of modulation by this method may be found in Schumann's Canon in B minor for pedal-piano (Op. 56, No. 5).

(*d*) The presence of suspensions and accented discords is always desirable, in moderation. A long note should, of course, be treated as a suspension (cf. E flat in bar 8, Ex. 140) and finally be forced to quit.

(*e*) The *free part* is not meant to meander. It should, of course, be the friend in need, supplying the essential notes which the canon is not using; but it should also be a part with a distinct character of its own, developing the opening phrase given to it, and it should be kept quite distinct from the canon in shape and rhythm until the coda arrives. Ex. 142–4 are the beginnings of three canons, designed to show how the character of the free part can be made a feature of the composition :—

Ex. 142.

Ex. 143.

Ex. 144.

Lento.

In Ex. 142, bar 6, the violin jumps *up* to C, whereas the 'cello jumped *down*; a legitimate and often useful device. At bar 9 the violin assumes the leadership, a change which adds interest and is worth bearing in mind. It would have been easy to continue the old arrangement by making bar 8 as follows :—

Ex. 145.

(6) The CODA should, above all, sound as if it were the natural and necessary ending to the whole. Too often an example is made to end, with a full close and tonic chord in its root-position all complete, and then a quite unnecessary and rambling addition of three or four bars destroys whatever feeling of finality had been secured. Every student knows how, in composing, in making up a short eight-bar example, in extemporizing—no less than in making a speech or writing a letter—there arrives a point at which the mind swings round and focusses on the final chord. The object after that point

is to avoid abruptness in leaving off, and to make it appear the inevitable end, without obviously breaking the vein of thought. This swinging-point is where the coda begins.

(7) A very useful and natural form of coda is the dominant pedal (see Ex. 140). In three-part writing it is a convention that the pedal does not count as a part : e.g. the last six bars of Ex. 140 are in four parts. The reason for this convention is simply the unsatisfactory thinness of sound when two parts bustle about over a stationary bass.

On a pedal there should be some definite business going on, generally some new treatment of old material. In Ex. 140 it will be seen that the *stretto* is used, the first phrase being answered at a distance of two beats instead of three. Ex. 146 is a pedal-coda to Ex. 142 : —

Ex. 146.

This, as will be seen, has two strettos, first at the distance of two quavers, then only one ; the third note of the alto is purposely made D instead of E to show that, as has been insisted on previously, *exactness* of imitation is no virtue.

One other point is worth noticing in Ex. 146. It is rather longer than codas to short canons need be, and specially long for a pedal-coda; consequently the monotony of the actual pedal note is a little mitigated by the quasi-syncopation of the latter half.

Ex. 147 is a coda, without pedal, to Ex. 144 :—

Ex. 147.

The fault in this coda is that it takes as its basis the rather naïve phrase of the opening, which has probably been overworked by the time the coda is reached : its excuse is that there was not much else to take, and that dullness is redeemed by the references in the bass to the free part, and the minim rests.

EXERCISES.

Continue the following canons for about sixteen bars, ending with a short coda :—

1.

For Violin, Viola, and 'Cello.

7.

8.

Continue the following, for about sixteen bars with coda, adding in each case your own free part:—

PART V

GROUND BASSES

CHAPTER XI

(1) A GROUND BASS is an unfigured bass which has to be repeated a given number of times *with varied treatment*. It is necessary to lay stress on the last three words, because the whole object of repetition in any form of art is the deliberate increasing, or abating, of emotion. Consequently the first law of a ground bass is that, supposing it is set in ten different ways, these ten versions should be presented in an order which leads from simple to complex, or from complex to simple, or from simple to a central climax and thence to a simple end, or vice versa. No haphazard arrangement can be artistic; not even (owing to the shortness of the subject and the consequent transitoriness of each mood) the method, frequently used with variations, of placing, say, a slow and mournful version between two rhythmical and militant ones.

(2) Before setting to work the bass should be exhaustively analysed, so that all of its possibilities may be utilized in at least one of the versions. The two following basses, of simple but different character, will be used for examples :—

(*a*) First determine what chances there are for modulation. In Bass A we can touch the following :—

Bar 1—G major.

Bar 2—A minor, F major, D minor, F minor.

Bar 3— „ „ „ „

Bar 4—F major (by means of a B flat carried on till F arrives again in the bass).

It is also possible, for the more elaborate versions, to suggest E major (by following the chord of E in bar 2 by an augmented 6th on F), and D flat major (by using both crotchets F as part of a chord of D flat).

Bass B does not lend itself so readily to modulation ; but the following are obvious :—

Bar 2—A major.

Bar 3—C major, F major, A minor.

Bar 4—C major, F major, E flat major (for Neapolitan 6th).

Also, by beginning with the chord of F, followed by a $^6_5$ on B♮; C major can be touched on at the start ; and for a point of colour, the minim D might once be used for a cadence in D major, with skill. And it is just conceivable, in a very modern version, that the last three minims might be driven into A flat major.

All possible, or all reasonable, modulations should be used somewhere, and it will be good practice to arrange the possible combinations so that no two versions have precisely the same key-scheme.

(*b*) Make a mental note of possible pedals, inverted and otherwise. Bass A will stand a dominant pedal above or below it ; also, for at least three bars, a tonic pedal. With management it is possible to use above it, until the last crotchet, a double pedal, tonic and mediant ; but such would be pointless if long tied notes were used. The last two variations in Bach's great organ Passacaglia show that a pedal is none the less authentic because it is worked into semiquaver figures :—

J. S. BACH.

(c) See if a canon is possible. It is often desirable, when at least two parts are full of movement, that the third should help the bass in sustaining equilibrium ; and if it can be canonic the interest is so much the greater. Bass B will go in canon at the octave, one bar distance ; inverted, one minim distance, &c. Ex. 148–51 show four versions of free canons (and dozens more are possible) which would be far better than mere 'filling up' of the alto.

Ex. 148.

Ex. 149.

Ex. 150.

Ex. 151.

(3) The different ways in which a bass may be treated are many in number, and twelve of the most usual ones will now be considered. The student is warned, for his own sake, not to learn this list by heart under the impression that it is exhaustive and binding. There are many other methods possible, and the mental exercise involved in thinking of some of them should be of real value to him. It may be taken for granted that ground basses are seldom intended to be vocal, but should be worked for strings or organ. The twelve methods of treatment suggested for practice at an early stage are as follows :—

(a) Simple harmony.
(b) Simple melodic phrases.
(c) Simple rhythmical figures.
(d) More elaborate harmony.
(e) More elaborate figures and phrases.
(f) Canons on the bass.
(g) Independent canons over the bass.
(h) Suspensions and appoggiaturas.
(i) Pedals.
(j) Putting the bass in the melody.
(k) Variation of the bass.
(l) Modern harmony (see ch. vi, § 14).

(a) *Simple harmony* does not mean something which sounds like a simple harmony exercise. Ex. 152 is the sort of version which constantly occurs, but it is inexcusable. Ex. 153 is a far better type :—

Ex. 152. (Bad.)

Ex. 153.

(*b*) By '*simple melodic phrases*' is meant the contrapuntal treatment of short tunes, such as one would use, with harmonic treatment, under (*a*) :—

Ex. 154.

(*c*) Ex. 155 shows how a *rhythmical figure* of an ingenuous kind can be taken and worked, to one's heart's content, round a bass. Of course, Bass A is of an elementary nature, but with a little ingenuity a simple figure can be worked into every beat of any bass :—

Ex. 155. (Bad.)

The above is marked 'bad' because, if the empty beats were filled up, and the whole offered as a 'version', it *would* be bad. There is too much in the window, and nothing worth looking at. Ex. 156 is an improvement :—

Ex. 156. (Poor.)

It is marked 'poor' because it is too obviously symmetrical. The 'tag' of Ex. 155 has been improved into a more musical phrase, but its persistence on the third beat, coupled with the bare harmonic interest, is unsatisfactory.

Ex. 157.

Ex. 157 improves on Ex. 156 by adding to its interest as harmony, and by shifting, in bars 3 and 4, the rhythmical interest from the third beat to the second. As an example of 'simple rhythmical figures' it is the kind of result which ought to emanate from the original profusion of Ex. 155.

(*d*) Smooth *harmonic writing* is occasionally desirable, both to show the possibilities of the bass and as a contrast to the more restless contrapuntal versions. At the beginning such writing should be on a simple chord basis, but when occurring later more enterprise should be shown, as in Ex. 158.

Ex. 158.

The extra beat has been printed at the beginning to show that it is often musicianly to make a new figure grow out of the cadence of the previous version.

(*e*) Just as (*d*) implies a more advanced treatment of the bass than (*a*) but on the same principles, so (*e*) implies a combination of (*b*) and (*c*) with more energy and sustained interest :—

Ex. 159.

(*f*) *Canons on the bass* are not difficult to work, so far as the mere canon is concerned ; but it is always necessary to keep the free parts from being dull.　If they can find nothing to say beyond the pointless filling up of chords, then the canon is not worth doing.　The student may be reminded that no attempt should be made to reproduce the exact semitones of the subject.　No fault can be found with Ex. 161 on the ground that F–G in the antecedent are answered by B flat and B natural in the consequent.

Ex. 160.

Ex. 161.

(g) An *independent canon* over the bass is often effective ; but must not be thought to acquire merit if it is quite uninteresting. It should not be too ingenuously simple, and suspensions and rests should be freely used, since the solidity of the bass gives a firm foundation which is lacking to the ordinary canon. The free part gets less scope here, since when three parts are given, the fourth part has a restricted channel open to it ; but care should be taken that it has something at all events worth phrasing :—

Ex. 162.

(*h*) *Suspensions* of all kinds, single, double, and treble, including retardations, should be used ; they seldom need a special version, since they naturally find their way into the settings in which some other device is the main feature.   Also, it is generally more interesting to treat them in the form of accented appoggiaturas.   In this latter case strict part writing may always be ignored in writing for the organ, and when strings are used double-stopping is permissible in moderation :—

Ex. 163.

In the above the first phrase might obviously have been written an octave lower, but it is often worth while, especially with longer basses, to suggest an antiphonal effect.

(*i*) Pedals have been dealt with in previous chapters : but it is worth pointing out that they need not necessarily extend the whole length of the bass, nor be in the same part continuously, nor even the same note (e. g. in Bass B the first eight crotchet-beats might have a dominant pedal in the alto, the next eight a tonic pedal in the treble).   So little enterprise is generally shown in the matter of pedals that the student may be reminded that unexpected notes are often the most effective for the purpose :—

Ex. 164.

(*j*) Placing the *melody in the treble* is an excellent way of relieving the monotony inherent in this form of composition. When the model is repeated many times it is always advisable to resort to this device, and it is also permissible to insert an occasional accidental (cf. F sharp in the melody of Ex. 165), not by way of avoiding any difficulty, but in order to touch some desirable key which cannot be reached when the model is in the bass :—

Ex. 165.

(*k*) Another way of avoiding monotony is to alter the note-values of the bass. When writing for the organ, where the continual use of the pedals becomes so wearisome, this method is constantly used ; and even in short examples, when the value of such a version as composition does not warrant its insertion, the student is advised to write the bass occasionally for the left hand, allowing the pedals to be silent.

Ex. 166.

(*l*) In using *modern harmony* the student is advised to think of big and unexpected discords, reserving the chromatic element for the passing notes. As this treatment is generally reserved for the climax it is well to bear in mind that the doubling of parts (to avoid thinness of tone) is always permissible, especially when writing for the organ. Ex. 167, for instance, is little more than a doubled version of the plain four-part writing in Ex. 168.

Ex. 167.

&c.

Ex. 168.

(4) The student is strongly advised to think out for himself other methods of treating basses. Every kind of device that has an idea behind it is legitimate. The bass may be repeated, for instance, on different degrees of the scale. Bass A might thus be used with A as its first note, then with F, &c. The bass itself may be inverted ; augmentation and diminution may be employed ; it may be placed in an inner part ; it may have accidentals put in—e. g. in Bass A the second note might, in one version, be D sharp, and the sixth F sharp. As a study in possibilities the well-known Passacaglia in Rheinberger's sonata in E minor, No. 8 (Op. 132), is beyond praise ; whilst the great C minor Passacaglia of Bach is, of course, unique.

(5) The CODA has been dealt with in ch. x, § 6. The same remarks apply, *mutatis mutandis*, to the coda to ground basses. Ex. 169 and 170 suggest codas to Basses A and B :—

Ex. 169.

Ex. 170.

(6) In collecting together the various versions, and welding them into a whole, the great thing is to choose the right order in the organic sense, so that a feeling of development shall pervade the result. The joins must be carefully managed, so that a sense of continuity may be preserved; and where possible it is musicianly to make a new phrase grow out of the old cadence. Ex. 171–3 are three complete Passacaglias. Ex. 171 is a short and simple one in three parts. Ex. 172 and 173 are the results of placing together the various versions of Basses A and B worked out in this chapter.

PASSACAGLIA FOR ORGAN.

Ex. 171.[1]

[1] From the author's book *The Organ.* Printed by kind permission of Messrs. Stainer & Bell.

PASSACAGLIA FOR ORGAN.

PASSACAGLIA FOR ORGAN.

Ex. 173.

EXERCISES.

Write not less than six versions of the following:—

PRINTED IN
GREAT BRITAIN
AT THE
UNIVERSITY PRESS
OXFORD
BY
JOHN JOHNSON
PRINTER
TO THE
UNIVERSITY